CIVIL ENGINEERING

AND THE Science of Structures

Crabtree Publishing Company

www.crabtreebooks.com

Andrew Solway

Crabtree Publishing Company

www.crabtreebooks.com

Author: Andrew Solway
Publishing plan research and development:
  Sean Charlebois, Reagan Miller
  Crabtree Publishing Company
Photo research: James Nixon
Editors: Paul Humphrey, Adrianna Morganelli,
  James Nixon
Proofreader: Kathy Middleton
Layout design: sprout.uk.com
Cover design and logo: Margaret Amy Salter
**Production coordinator and prepress
  technician:** Margaret Amy Salter
Print coordinator: Katherine Berti

Produced for Crabtree Publishing Company
by Discovery Books

Photographs:
Alamy: pp. 11 (Rolf Richardson), 15 middle (Nino
  Marcutti), 18 (Focus Technology),
  22 (Prisma Bildagentur AG), 23 top (John
  Henshall), 23 bottom (VIEW Pictures Ltd).
Corbis: pp. 6 (Bettmann), 13 (Michael S.
  Yamashita), 17 (AStock), 20 (Viviane Moos),
  24 (Bettmann), 28 (Sergei Ilnitsky/EPA).
LOCOG: pp. 9 top (Dave Poultney), 9 bottom
  (Anthony Charlton).
Shutterstock: cover (all except top and bottom
  right), pp. 4 (Dmitry Kalinovsky), 7 top (Ramon
  Espelt Photography), 7 bottom (Jessmine), 8 (Lev
  Kropotov), 10 (Dmitry Pistrov), 12 (Wavebreak-
  media), 15 top (Darren J. Bradley), 15 bottom
  (Radoslaw Lecyk), 21 (leungchopan), 26 top-left
  (Crepesoles), 26 top-right (Amnartk), 26 bottom-
  left (design56), 26 bottom-right (Igor A. Bon-
  darenko), 27 (Alex Cofaru), 29 (Orhan Cam).
Thinkstock: cover (top and bottom right)
Wikimedia: pp. 5 (Hantsheroes), 25 (Emanuele
  Paolini).

Library and Archives Canada Cataloguing in Publication

Solway, Andrew
     Civil engineering and the science of structures / Andrew Solway.

(Engineering in action)
Includes index.
Issued also in electronic formats.
ISBN 978-0-7787-7496-9 (bound).--ISBN 978-0-7787-7501-0 (pbk.)

     1. Civil engineering--Juvenile literature. 2. Buildings--Juvenile
literature. I. Title. II. Series: Engineering in action (St. Catharines,
Ont.)

TA149.S65 2012   j624   C2012-906843-8

Library of Congress Cataloging-in-Publication Data

CIP available at Library of Congress

Crabtree Publishing Company

Printed in Canada/102013/MA20130906

www.crabtreebooks.com   1-800-387-7650

Published in Canada
Crabtree Publishing
616 Welland Ave.
St. Catharines, ON
L2M 5V6

Published in the United States
Crabtree Publishing
PMB 59051
350 Fifth Avenue, 59th Floor
New York, New York 10118

Published in the United Kingdom
Crabtree Publishing
Maritime House
Basin Road North, Hove
BN41 1WR

Published in Australia
Crabtree Publishing
3 Charles Street
Coburg North
VIC, 3058

CONTENTS

WHAT IS CIVIL ENGINEERING?

Nearly all the structures around us are made by civil engineers. Civil engineers shape our environment. They can build skyscrapers over a hundred stories high and bridges that span great rivers. They build dams that provide water and electricity for millions of people. They cut tunnels under city streets and below the seabed. They build railways across deserts, roads, and through mountain ranges.

Even the smaller things that civil engineers build are important, such as drains that keep cities free from disease, or sea walls that protect the coast from floods.

An engineer uses an instrument called a theodolite to map out a building site. Theodolites use lasers to measure distances.

Engineering and science:
Engineering and science are closely linked—but they are not the same thing. Scientists are interested in understanding the world as it exists. They do experiments and make discoveries. Engineers are more interested in shaping the world to meet human needs. They want to find useful solutions to practical problems.

Let's look at lasers to see the different approaches of science and engineering. Scientists use lasers to investigate the world. For example, they might shine a laser through a sample of a material and measure how the light changes. This can provide information about the structure of the material. Engineers use lasers to measure distances and angles.

Eight steps to success: Today civil engineers follow a well-established process to ensure designs for structures are the best and safest they can be. They follow an eight-step process to design, build, and test new designs:

Identify the problem

↓

Identify criteria and constraints

↓

Brainstorm possible solutions

↓

Select a design

↓

Build a model or prototype

Test the model and evaluate → **Refine the design**

↓

Share the solution

SIR SANDFORD FLEMING

Sir Sandford Fleming worked from the age of 22 as a **surveyor** and engineer on the Canadian Railways. The railways that he built created a transport network that helped to unite the provinces of Canada into a single country.

During his work on the railways, Fleming realized that there was a problem keeping the trains on time. Different parts of Canada kept their own local time. So Fleming changed local timekeeping into a series of time zones across the country. This was later extended to become the worldwide system of time zones used today.

A wall painting shows
Sir Sandford Fleming
in Halifax, Nova Scotia.

GREAT STRUCTURES OF THE PAST

The people who built the Egyptian pyramids, the Great Wall of China, and medieval cathedrals were not called engineers. They were craftspeople such as stonemasons, carpenters, or master builders. But in fact, these people *were* civil engineers. They used a mixture of tried and tested methods and new ideas in building these great structures. Often they built test designs to see if a new idea would work.

There has been great debate about how the pyramids were built. The stone blocks may have been dragged, lifted, or even rolled into place.

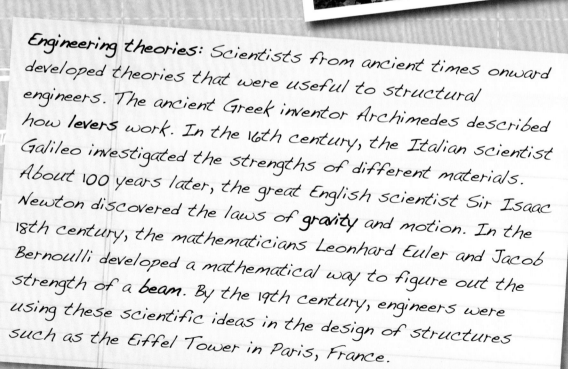

Engineering theories: Scientists from ancient times onward developed theories that were useful to structural engineers. The ancient Greek inventor Archimedes described how **levers** work. In the 16th century, the Italian scientist Galileo investigated the strengths of different materials. About 100 years later, the great English scientist Sir Isaac Newton discovered the laws of **gravity** and motion. In the 18th century, the mathematicians Leonhard Euler and Jacob Bernoulli developed a mathematical way to figure out the strength of a **beam**. By the 19th century, engineers were using these scientific ideas in the design of structures such as the Eiffel Tower in Paris, France.

Civil engineering also advanced because of the development of new materials. In the 19th century, new methods were developed for producing iron, steel, and concrete cheaply. A French gardener named Joseph Monier came up with the idea of reinforced concrete, where steel mesh is put inside concrete to make it stronger. Toward the end of the 19th century, structures such as the Forth Rail Bridge in Scotland showed that iron and steel could be used to build bigger, stronger structures. In the early 20th century, Robert Maillot was a **pioneer** in the use of reinforced concrete in bridges.

When the Forth Rail Bridge was completed in 1890, it was the world's first large steel bridge.

THE DOME AT FLORENCE (BUILT 1419-1445)

The cathedral in Florence, Italy, has the biggest brick dome ever built. The dome design had no **buttresses** to support it from the outside, and it was too high and wide to be supported by scaffolding while it was being built. The **architect** Filippo Brunelleschi found ingenious solutions to all the challenges of building this huge structure. He stopped the dome from spreading outward with four iron and stone chains running right around the dome. He prevented the top of the dome from falling in as it was built by using a herringbone brick pattern in which the bricks locked together and held the structure in place. He designed and built a giant crane and several other machines that could lift the brick and stone up to the height of the dome.

MODERN ENGINEERS

A modern civil engineering project involves the skills of many different people. The civil engineers are at the center of the process. They work with people such as designers and architects, builders, plumbers, electricians, and many others.

A team effort: On a large project, there are many different types of civil engineers. Some study the geology (the structure of the rocks) in an area, to be sure that the ground will be able to support the structure. Some are specialists in materials—they decide what materials will work best for different parts of the structure. A team of engineers create the overall design of the structure and design the separate parts. Then there are on-site engineers who check that the work is built to the plan and solve problems that come up along the way. All civil engineers need to be good at math and science, but they also need to be practical and good problem-solvers.

Site engineers help to sort out the day-to-day issues that come up when building any large structure.

An Olympic roof

The Aquatics Centre for the 2012 London Olympics was an engineering challenge because the roof is a series of complex curves, and is supported at only three points. The building was designed by architect Zaha Hadid. Turning the designs into a practical building was the job of the civil engineers on the project. The engineers worked with the architects to decide what kind of materials to use, how to make the roof strong enough to support its own weight, and how to construct the roof on site.

Before construction could begin, **geologists** had to check that the ground was stable enough to hold the structure, and surveyors prepared the site for building. The engineers had to **collaborate** with all these people as well as the builders to make sure that the construction went smoothly.

The Olympic Aquatics Centre in London. The top picture shows how the roof was supported in only three places when it was being built.

The engineers worked with a steel firm in South Wales who built the roof supports, and with a German company who made the aluminum roof covering. The finished roof weighed 3,086 tons (2,800 metric tons) and was 525 feet (160 meters) long. While it was being built, the roof framework was supported on a set of temporary **trestles**. Partway through construction one set of trestles had to be removed so that work on digging out the swimming pools could begin. Once the roof framework was complete, it was lifted off the trestles and lowered onto its three permanent supports.

THE ENGINEERING PROCESS

Suppose a civil engineer has to create a **junction** where two roads meet. Should it be an intersection with traffic lights? One road going over the other? Or would a roundabout be best? Even such a small engineering problem can have large consequences. The wrong decision could lead to years of traffic gridlock.

When engineers start a new project, they go through a series of steps to try to find the best solution for the situation. The whole process is a cycle that can happen again and again, to improve and refine the design.

This complex junction of many roads in Tel Aviv, Israel, needed a creative engineering solution.

Identify the problem: The first stage in a civil engineering project is to clearly set out the job that needs to be done. For example, one of the biggest civil engineering projects of the 20th century was the construction of a new airport for Hong Kong. Hong Kong's existing airport, Kai Tak, was too small to handle all the passengers and air freight coming in and out of the city. It was in the middle of a heavily populated area, which caused safety concerns. It was also in an awkward place, which made it difficult for aircraft to take off and land. The challenge was to build a bigger airport, where large aircraft could approach and land safely.

Identify criteria and constraints: The second step in the engineering design process is to identify constraints. These are things that have to be taken into account when looking for a solution to the engineering problem. An example is cost—nearly all projects have limits to the amount of money that can be spent. The location could be a constraint. For example, the structure may have to look a certain way to fit in with historic buildings or an area of great natural beauty. There may be constraints due to the geology of the area (the structure of the rocks). For example, there could be soft or waterlogged ground, or earthquake activity in the area. Environmental concerns could also be a constraint. For example, a building might need to have low carbon **emissions.**

In the case of the Hong Kong airport project, the biggest constraint was lack of land. Hong Kong itself is an island crowded with skyscrapers. The nearby mainland is also densely populated. Over 40 percent of the region is mountainous and covered with forest. There was no flat land where aircraft could take off and land safely.

Airliners landing at Kai Tak, Hong Kong's old airport, had to fly low over densely populated areas. A crash landing would have been a major disaster.

BRAINSTORMING

The third stage in the engineering design process is an important one—come up with some ideas! Brainstorming means coming up with lots of ideas in a short space of time. Even wild or impractical ideas are included. At this stage the aim is simply to have a lot of different ideas. Each one can be assessed at a later stage in the process.

One of the possible solutions to the problem of a lack of flat land for Hong Kong airport seemed very wild. The idea was to flatten two small, mountainous islands not far from Hong Kong Island, and join them together in one large artificial (man-made) island.

In a brainstorming meeting any idea can be discussed, no matter how strange it might seem!

Generate ideas: This is the stage at which engineers look at the ideas from the brainstorming process and see if they could be part of a practical idea. Several ideas from the brainstorming process could come together into a possible solution. Or it might be possible to look at one promising idea and develop it into a good solution.

Although it seemed ridiculous at first, engineers looked carefully at the idea of creating an artificial island base for the new Hong Kong airport. It was a difficult and expensive solution, but it was possible. They developed the idea further by thinking about exactly how two high, rocky islands could be turned into one larger, flat island. They also looked at weather conditions around the islands. Hong Kong suffers regularly from typhoons, with winds of over 200 mph (300 kph). How well would an airport on a flat island in the sea survive such winds?

The artificial island is shown here during construction of the new Hong Kong airport. The island was made very flat, to provide a good area for airliners to land.

MAKING NEW LAND

How do you build an artificial island? In the case of Hong Kong airport, two steep islands had to be turned into one flat one. To achieve this, engineers used explosives to blast away the hills on the islands. This produced huge mounds of rocky rubble. Next, the muddy seabed between the two islands was **dredged** down to rock to provide a solid base for the new area of land. Finally, the millions of tons of rubble were bulldozed into the water between the two islands to lift the level of the land above sea level, joining the islands.

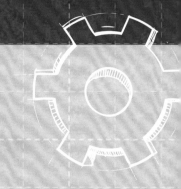

EXPLORING POSSIBILITIES

At this stage a few possible solutions have been identified. These are now shared and discussed more widely, to try to decide which is the best solution to take forward.

For the Hong Kong airport project, engineers had a workable solution for the airport itself—build an artificial island. However, if the airport was built in this location it would be completely isolated. Would it be possible to build transportation links to connect the new airport to the city?

Connecting the new airport to the center of Hong Kong would involve building over 22 miles (35 kilometers) of new road and rail links. The route would cross two stretches of sea that were one mile (1.6 km) wide and three miles (five km) wide. The first stretch of water, under Victoria Harbour, already had a road tunnel running under it. Engineers decided that the best way to cross this sea was probably another tunnel. The second stretch of water, crossing to Lantau Island, was a busy sea lane for ships. Building a tunnel through this would be very disruptive. Could a bridge be a better solution?

Different bridges
There are various types of bridge design. Each one has advantages and disadvantages. Some of the most important types are shown on these pages.

Beam bridge: This can be as simple as a plank over a stream. Each part of the bridge is basically a beam resting on two or more supports. They are cheap and easy to build over short spans.

Arch bridge: An arch bridge can span a wider gap than a beam bridge. Concrete arch bridges are often used to span high valleys.

Cable-stayed bridge: A newer type of bridge in which the bridge **deck** is suspended from cables connected to a high support tower. This kind of bridge can span wide gaps. Most of the load (the weight that the bridge can support) is carried by the support towers.

Suspension bridge: This kind of bridge can cross the widest gaps. Two very long cables span the gap and are held firmly in place at both ends. The cables run between two high support towers. The deck of the bridge is hung from these two cables using a series of short supporting cables. The main load is shared by the support towers and the anchor points.

SELECTING AN APPROACH

If a bridge is used to carry road and rail transportation, what would be the best design for the crossing to Lantau Island?

✔ The total crossing from Tsin Yi Island to Lantau Island is about three miles (five km).

✔ In between the two large islands is another island, Ma Wan. The Ma Wan Channel, on the east side, is about 1.6 miles (two km) wide and is a busy sea lane.

✔ The channel on the west side of the island is about 1,475 feet (450 m) wide. This channel is also a busy shipping lane.

✔ Any bridge will have to be able to survive the typhoon winds that blow through the channel.

Look back at the descriptions of the different bridge types on the previous page. Which of them might work for the Lantau Island crossing? Why do you think this would be the best choice?

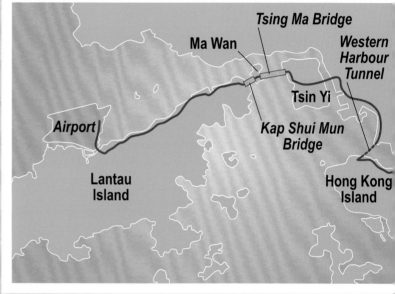

This map shows the main transportation route from the center of Hong Kong to the new airport. Building it involved digging a three-lane tunnel, building three very long bridges, and creating new land along the coast of Lantau Island.

Two different types of bridges were constructed on either side of Ma Wan Island.

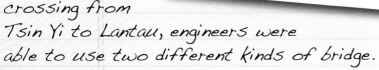

Making a choice: Because Ma Wan Island is in the middle of the crossing from Tsin Yi to Lantau, engineers were able to use two different kinds of bridge.

- Over the wide stretch from Tsin Yi to Ma Wan, they suggested using a suspension bridge. Suspension bridges can span the widest gaps.

- Over the narrower channel from Ma Wan to Lantau, they suggested using a cable-stayed bridge. This bridge needs less cable and can be built faster than a suspension bridge.

VITAL STATISTICS

Two bridges were built across the channel from Tsin Yi to Lantau Island. They are connected by a 1,650-foot (503 m) viaduct that runs across Ma Wan Island.

Tsing Ma Bridge
- Opened May 22, 1997
- Length: 7,087 feet (2160 m)
- Longest span: 4,518 feet (1,377 m)
- Height above water: 203 ft (62 m)
- Width: 135 feet (41 m); wide enough for a six-lane highway.

Kap Shui Mun Bridge
- Opened May 22, 1997
- Length 2,460 feet (750 m)
- Longest span: 1,475 feet (430 m)
- Height above water: 154 feet (47 m)
- Width: 123 feet (32.5 m)

BUILDING PROTOTYPES

After assessing a few possible solutions to a problem, the engineers then pick one solution and build a prototype. This is a model that can be tested to see how the actual structure is likely to react.

Today's civil engineers do most of their design work using computers. Computer-aided design systems can be run on a tablet computer.

Testing the prototype: Once engineers had decided that the Tsing Ma Bridge should be a suspension bridge, they first tested a **computer model**. The computer model showed how much the bridge might move in the strong winds and where the strongest **forces** acted on it.

Next, the engineers built a **scale model** of the bridge design and tested it in a **wind tunnel**. The results of these tests showed that the deck moved about in the wind far more than expected. What was the best way to solve the problem? Would the engineers have to completely alter the design, or even abandon it altogether?

FORCES

In civil engineering, engineers have to take into account all the forces that act on a structure, then make sure that it can cope with them.

Gravity is an important force in civil engineering. A bridge, building, or other structure has to be strong enough to support its own weight against the force of gravity.

Gravity is a **static force**: it does not change. It is relatively easy to design a structure to withstand static forces. Other forces are **dynamic** and are harder to predict. Examples are the movements of traffic across a bridge, wind blowing against a building, or waves crashing into a seawall.

Forces have different effects on different parts of a structure. The supports holding up a roof are under compression. That means they are pressed down by the weight of the roof. The cables that support the deck of a suspension bridge are under tension. That means the ends are being pulled in opposite directions. A heavy weight on a beam produces bending forces. The top of the beam is compressed, while the bottom is under tension. Torsion is a twisting force, like in the shaft of a wind turbine. Shear forces occur when one end of a structure is pushed one way and the other end is pushed in the opposite direction.

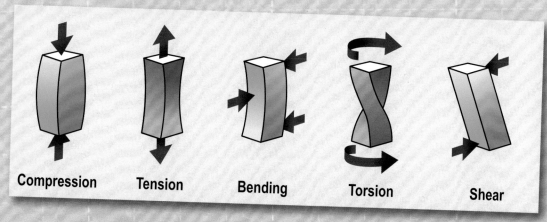

Compression   Tension   Bending   Torsion   Shear

These are the five main types of force that can act on a structure.

IMPROVING THE DESIGN

Prototype testing almost always shows up faults that have to be corrected before a final design can be chosen and built. Sometimes prototype tests may show that the design will not be a solution to the problem after all. It may be necessary to go back and try an alternative solution.

This image shows an early stage in the construction of the Tsing Ma Bridge. The hollow construction of the bridge deck allows for two separate levels, one for trains and one for cars.

A MASSIVE PROJECT

The two bridges and viaduct built to link the city of Hong Kong to the new airport used a massive 220,500 tons (200,000 metric tons) of concrete. The length of wire used in the bridges' cables measured about 100,000 miles (160,000 km)—enough to circle the world four times!

Try out the design process: How strong a bridge could you build from six kitchen roll tubes and some corrugated cardboard? Use the tubes for the bridge supports and the cardboard to make the deck. Go through the stages of the engineering design process to come up with the best design. Which design gives you the strongest bridge? Can you think of a way to make it stronger?

Get some friends to make their own designs and see which one is the strongest. For this to be a fair test, you all have to use the same amount of cardboard, and the bridges all have to span the same distance.

In most cases there will be several cycles of building a prototype, testing it, and then improving the design based on the test results. Once the flaws in the prototype have been corrected, the design can be finalized. It is ready to be built! When engineers found that the deck of the Tsing Ma Bridge moved a lot in high winds, they made major changes to the design. The edges of the deck were **tapered,** so the wind flowed more smoothly over and under it. They also made vent holes in the sides to allow some air to pass through the deck. These changes greatly reduced the movement of the deck in strong winds.

The completed Tsing Ma Bridge is shown here at night.

REAL-LIFE SOLUTIONS

The engineering design process is a powerful tool for finding solutions to real-life engineering problems. Here are some solutions from real projects.

MOVING THE RIVER

The Itaipu Dam between Brazil and Paraguay in South America is one of the biggest in the world. It was built in the 1970s across the Parana River. The river had to be diverted through a channel that took three years to dig. Once the water was flowing through this channel, giant temporary dams called cofferdams were built at either end of the original river channel. This stopped any water from flowing down the old riverbed and gave workers a dry area where they could build the dam.

This aerial view shows the massive scale of the Itaipu Dam complex.

Earthquake proofing: Up until 2010, the skyscraper Taipei 101, in Taiwan, was the tallest building in the world. But Taiwan is in an area where earthquakes and typhoons are common. To protect against earthquakes, the skyscraper had to be extremely stable. Thirty-six high-performance, steel columns support the structure, and its foundations reach nearly 100 feet (30 m) into the ground.

The surprising feature of the design is a giant steel ball weighing 730 tons (660 metric tons), which hangs from cables on the 92nd floor. The ball is a **mass damper**. When high winds or vibrations shake a tall building, the vibrations can build up until the top part sways violently from side to side. The steel ball swings the opposite way to the building itself, and this dampens down the vibrations.

The tallest bridge

At its highest point, the Millau Viaduct, in France, is 1,125 feet (343 m) from the top to the base. This makes it the tallest bridge in the world. Constructing the deck of the viaduct was a real problem. Lifting huge road sections over one thousand feet into the air is incredibly difficult and dangerous. So the engineers found a different solution. They built the deck from steel instead of concrete to make it lighter and stronger. The deck was built on the valley sides, then pushed out from either side towards the center. A set of **hydraulic rams** on the top of each pillar moved the roadway forwards by lifting it, inching it forward, then letting it down again. When the two sections met high over the valley, they were in line with each other to within half an inch (one cm).

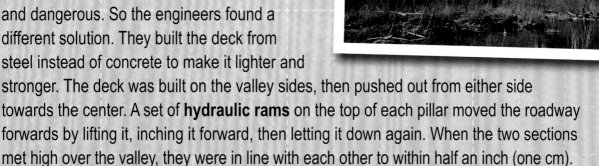

LEARNING FROM MISTAKES

Civil engineers build for the long term. The Eiffel Tower was only meant to last 20 years, but it has survived for over 120 years and is likely to stand for many more. But very occasionally, things go wrong. A building collapses, a tunnel caves in, or a bridge falls down. Engineers try to learn from such disasters and make sure they won't happen again.

The Tacoma Narrows Bridge
In 1940, a new suspension bridge was opened across the Tacoma Narrows in Puget Sound, Washington. The bridge was nicknamed "Galloping Gertie" because in windy conditions the deck rocked wildly. Four months after opening, the bridge deck began to move up and down in strong winds. then twist from side to side. Eventually the middle of the bridge collapsed. The only casualty was a small dog.

The first Tacoma Narrows Bridge in 1940, shortly after it collapsed in high winds.

The Tacoma bridge collapse showed the importance of testing how a bridge responds to wind. Suspension bridges built after the disaster had **trusses** along the sides to make the deck stiffer, and holes to let the wind could pass through the deck instead of pushing against it.

The Vajont Dam

The Vajont dam was built in a steep-sided mountain valley in the Italian Alps. When completed in 1960 it was the tallest dam in the world. Even before the dam was completed there were worries that the mountain slopes behind the reservoir were unstable. In late 1960, there was a small landslide on the south side of the valley.

Once the dam was built, it blocked the river's flow, and water gradually built up behind the dam wall. For three years the water level behind the dam slowly rose. Then in October 1963, a huge section of the valley fell into the reservoir. It pushed an enormous wave high up the opposite slope. The wave destroyed the village of Casso, 850 feet (260 m) above the reservoir. It then crashed over 1,600 feet (490 m) into the valley below the dam. Three villages were totally destroyed and over 2,000 people were killed. Amazingly, the dam itself remained intact.

The Vajont Dam wall is still intact and is maintained, but now there is no reservoir behind the dam wall.

PREPARING FOR THE WORST

The disaster at Vajont Dam was due to a poor survey of the land in the area before construction began. Today, no dam project begins without a proper survey by qualified engineers. In another example, earthquakes in Japan and California caused buildings to collapse. This led to the development of earthquake engineering.

DESIGN CHALLENGE

How are your engineering skills? Use the eight steps of the engineering design process to help you carry out this design challenge.

Using the materials provided, build a stable structure as tall as possible. The structure has to stand up in the breeze from an electric fan. The materials you can use for this challenge are:

100 wooden toothpicks
50 jelly candies
sewing thread
a lump of clay for the base

1: Identify the problem: Begin by setting out the problem clearly. Your aim is to build a tall, stable structure. The main constraints on your structure will be the strength and the quantity of materials that you have for building your structure.

2: Research the problem: If you are building with toothpicks and candies, your structure will have to be made from struts and joints. Look for examples of structures that are made this way. How do the struts and joints go together? You should also do some research into how skyscrapers and other tall structures are built.

3: Develop possible solutions: Sketch out several ideas for your structure. Make the sketches accurate in the details that you think are important, such as the angles at which parts join together and the amount of material used for the whole design.

4: Select the best solution or solutions: Look critically at the different ideas. What are the advantages and disadvantages of each one? Remember that the aim is to build a tall structure, but one that can stand up in "windy" conditions. Decide which design will work best.

5: Construct a prototype: Having decided which design to try, you need to test it out. A prototype is often a smaller version of the final structure, but in this case you may want to put part of your design together to test out whether your construction ideas work.

6: Test and evaluate the solution: Now build your complete design and test it in the "wind" from an electric fan. Is the structure stable? Does it use all the materials? Can you build it as high as you had planned? Evaluate the results of your tests. What worked? What didn't work?

7: Communicate your solution: At this stage you need to communicate your ideas. Put together a report on the design process, what ideas you came up with, and the results of your tests.

8: Redesign: Now go back and look at your design. If the tests showed that there were problems, can you find solutions? If the design basically worked, are there ways to improve it? Can you make it more stable? Could you use fewer materials in the design so that you could build the structure higher?

Look carefully at the way the Eiffel Tower is constructed. It may help you with the design of your tower.

INTO THE FUTURE

Civil engineering has changed enormously in the last 100 years. It is likely to change even more in the next 100 years. What sort of changes are we likely to see in the future?

New materials

New materials are beginning to replace materials such as steel and concrete. For example, the plastic ETFE is a transparent material that is lighter than glass and better at keeping in heat. The Eden Project in the UK is a series of huge domed greenhouses containing all kinds of different plants. The transparent domes of the greenhouse are made from ETFE, which is the ideal material for this purpose.

Other new materials are **composites**—a combination of fibers fixed in a plastic **resin**. The fibers provide strength and stiffness, and the plastic makes the material light and easy to shape. Smart materials are another exciting development that are beginning to be used in civil engineering. One development is "smart glass," which can change its transparency depending on the light levels or when electricity is passed through it. This can be used to make windows that darken in bright sunlight or that can be made dark by turning a switch.

Another smart material in the pipeline is self-healing concrete. It contains bacteria mixed with a special type of concrete. When a crack appears in the concrete, the bacteria grow into the space. The bacteria produce a waste that hardens like concrete and fills in the crack.

The beautiful white covering of the Cultural Center in Baku, Azerbaijan, is made from glass-fiber reinforced polymer (GFRP). It is strong and weighs less than a similar covering made from concrete.

Going green: The need to reduce energy use is now an important aim of many building projects. Some new skyscrapers and large office blocks, for instance, are built without air conditioning, which uses a lot of energy in most large buildings. Instead they use a system of tall chimneys and air passages that draw heat out at the top of the building and draw cool air in below. The idea for this kind of system came from studying the design of termite mounds!

The Bahrain World Trade Center in Manama, Bahrain, is a twin skyscraper connected by three bridges. On each of these bridges there is a large wind turbine. The three turbines provide about 10 percent of the electricity used by the skyscrapers.

BLOW-UP STRUCTURES

Everyone has tried out a bouncy castle, but what if you could live in one? Inflatable buildings are already used to provide temporary housing. For example, there are tents for **refugees** and large marquees for outdoor events, which are easy to erect. Inflatable technology could also be used in space. NASA is researching the use of inflatable solar panels that can be used by satellites to generate electricity in space.

LEARNING MORE

BOOKS

Barber, Nicola, *Buildings and Structures*, Heinemann Raintree, 2010

Brasch, Nicolas, *Amazing Built Structures*, Smart Apple Media, 2011

Ebner, Aviva, *Engineering Science Experiments*, Chelsea House, 2011

Latham, Donna and Vaughn, Jen, *Bridges and Tunnels: Investigate Feats of Engineering with 25 Projects*, Nomad Press, 2012

Miller, Ron, *Seven Wonders of Engineering*, Twenty-First Century Books, 2011

Priwer, Shana and Phillips, Cynthia, *Dams and Waterways*, M. E. Sharpe, 2009

Wolny, Philip, *High Risk Construction Work: Life Building Skyscrapers, Bridges, and Tunnels*, Rosen Central, 2008

ONLINE

www.pbs.org/wgbh/buildingbig/index.html
Interactive labs, engineering challenges, and fact files about the tallest, longest, heaviest, and strongest structures in the world

www.nationalgeographic.com/pyramids/pyramids.html.
Learn more about the ancient Egyptian pyramids and how they were built.

www.mtc.ca.gov/news/info/movies/sas_erection.htm.
How do you build a huge bridge tower offshore? This simulation shows the building of one of the towers of the San Francisco-Oakland Bay Bridge.

www.youtube.com/watch?v=j-zczJXSxnw
The collapse of the Tacoma Narrows Bridge in 1940 was captured on film. Watch it here!

http://kids.nationalgeographic.com/kids/stories/spacescience/snowfences/
This science fair engineering challenge turned into something really useful.

GLOSSARY

architect Someone who designs buildings

beam A long piece of steel, concrete, or other material that is used to span the gap between two vertical supports

buttresses Supports set at an angle against the wall of a building or a dam, that help stop the wall from bulging outward

collaborate To work together

composite A material made from two or more different materials combined together

computer model An electronic simulation of a structure that acts in a similar way to the real structure

deck The part of a bridge that carries the road, railway, or footpath

dredged Having dug out a river channel or other waterway to make it deeper

dynamic Moving

emissions Substances that are released into the air

forces Pushes, pulls, or twists

geologist A scientist who studies rocks and how the landscape was formed

gravity On Earth, gravity is a downward force that pulls everything toward the ground

hydraulic ram A machine that uses liquid under pressure to produce a strong pushing force

junction A place where two or more roads cross paths in a controlled way

lever A simple machine consisting of a straight bar that can turn freely around a fixed point, called the pivot. A force on one end of the lever produces a force on the opposite end.

mass damper Something very heavy that helps to damp down (reduce) the movements of a structure during an earthquake or a hurricane

pioneer The first person to develop an idea or technique

refugee A person who is forced to leave their home country to escape war or disaster

resin A material, often a plastic, that can be melted, then cools to a hard solid form

scale model A physical model of a structure built to a smaller or possibly larger scale

static forces Forces that are constant and do not change

surveyor A person who examines and records the features of an area of land, for the purpose of planning building work

tapered Something that gets thinner toward one end

trestle A framework of steel or other material used as a temporary support

truss A framework of struts, joined together in triangles that is used to strengthen or support a structure

viaduct A bridge-like structure that carries a road or railway across a valley

wind tunnel A tunnel with a large fan at one end that can be used to simulate the effects of wind on a bridge or other structure

INDEX